Josiah Henry Benton

Argument of J.H. Benton, Jr., Esq.,

before the Committee on Public Health of the Massachusetts Legislature:

against the petition of the Massachusetts Medical Society for the passage

of an act to regulate the practice of medicine

Josiah Henry Benton

Argument of J.H. Benton, Jr., Esq.,
before the Committee on Public Health of the Massachusetts Legislature: against the petition of the Massachusetts Medical Society for the passage of an act to regulate the practice of medicine

ISBN/EAN: 9783337152062

Printed in Europe, USA, Canada, Australia, Japan

Cover: Foto ©Suzi / pixelio.de

More available books at **www.hansebooks.com**

ARGUMENT

OF

J. H. BENTON, JR., ESQ.,

BEFORE

THE COMMITTEE ON PUBLIC HEALTH OF THE MASSACHUSETTS LEGISLATURE

AGAINST THE

PETITION OF THE MASSACHUSETTS MEDICAL SOCIETY

FOR THE PASSAGE OF AN ACT TO REGULATE THE PRACTICE OF MEDICINE.

STATE HOUSE, BOSTON, MARCH 6, 1885.

WRIGHT & POTTER PRINTING CO., STATE PRINTERS, 18 POST OFFICE SQ., BOSTON.

ARGUMENT OF J. H. BENTON, Jr., Esq.

This is the petition of the Massachusetts Medical Society for " An Act to Regulate the Practice of Medicine " in Massachusetts. It raises an important question. It raises a question which touches the personal happiness and security of every man, woman and child in this Commonwealth, and time which is spent in considering it fully is not wasted,

I desire to invite your attention to the history of the legislation upon this subject in this Commonwealth, but first I want to say a few words about the petition and the proposed bill. It appears that last June the Massachusetts Medical Society appointed a committee of seventeen, — I take it one from each of the seventeen districts in the State, — to prepare a bill upon this subject and to procure its enactment by this legislature. In pursuance of that a bill was prepared, and a circular, which I will now read, was sent over the State : —

"DEAR DOCTOR : — Herewith find a copy of a bill, prepared after very careful consideration by a committee appointed by the Massachusetts Medical Society, at their annual meeting last June.

It will be observed that it is based upon no society or class distinction, but upon the evidence of possession of a fundamental knowledge of the science of medicine."

Well, if the members of the Massachusetts Medical Society are willing to stand upon the claim that the examination provided for in this bill goes to a fundamental knowledge of the science of medicine, when they have left therapeutics and *Materia Medica* out of it absolutely, they take a much more narrow view in the law than they do in their own standard for examination for admission to their own body.

"It has been framed with the thought only of the protection of the people from fraud and ignorance, and has had the almost unanimous approval of the best men consulted in the profession, regardless of modes of practice.

Twenty-six States have already taken action upon this important subject, and a number of others are now pressing action in their respective legislatures. It is believed that the present presents certain marked advantages for the securing of legislation."

Just what those marked advantages are I don't know; perhaps some people can surmise.

"This circular is addressed, as far as possible, to every member of the medical and dental profession within the State, and your committee earnestly hope you will *at once* return to the secretary your approval of its passage."

There is a direct call to each member of the medical and dental profession in Massachusetts to return at once his approval of this bill.

"And *write* briefly to your *representative* your reasons therefor. You can be of great service in doing this, but *only by immediate* action.

Very respectfully,

HENRY O. MARCY, *Sec'y of Committee.*

116 Boylston Street, Boston, Feb. 13, 1835."

That bill, for some unknown reason, has not been openly presented to this committee, and yet every member has had a copy of it in his pocket. Everybody understands that it is the bill which the committee of the Massachusetts Medical Society wants; and I cannot understand why, unless they are ashamed of it, they have been unwilling to present it for fair and impartial discussion. There are, I believe, about 2,000 physicians in the three medical societies in Massachusetts, — about 1,600 in the Massachusetts Medical Society, about 300 in the Homœopathic Society, as I understand, and about 100 in the Eclectic. I don't know how many dental surgeons there are, but a good many. This bill, with a request for its approval, has been sent to every one of these gentlemen, and out of the whole number 168 only have returned any kind of an approval of its extraordinary provisions. (Applause.) Fifteen oppose it, and of the 161 who endorse it, — many of them by simply writing on the back of the circular, " I approve," which is not a very marked endorsement, — of the 161 who endorse it at all, 117 are members of the Massachusetts Medical Society. And of the twenty medical gentlemen who have appeared in favor of this bill, all but three are members of the Massachusetts Medical Society, and of that three, one, I believe, was a horse doctor. (Laughter.) He said to the members of the committee that he really did n't know what he did want. He had written a book of 400 pages, but he did n't think that ought to be enacted, although something ought to be done. Among these letters there is one from a member of the Massachusetts Medical Society who sits upon this committee ; and the chairman of this committee, who has presided with such uniform fairness and clearness, is a member of that society.

I am not here to say anything against that ancient and able organization. It was created at a time when there was but one school of medicine, and it was given extraordinary powers, and it exercised them from 1788 to 1860 as wisely and as well as any exclusive body of men from one particular school of a profession probably could exercise such powers. But I invite your consideration for a few moments to the history of the legislation in this State on this subject : because it is wise, when you are asked to enact a new law, to see whether there has been any law on that subject before, and how it has worked, and what the people have done with it.

The Massachusetts Medical Society was incorporated in 1781. (Laws of Mass., vol. III., pp. 140, 145.) It was given corporate powers ; authorized to sue and to be sued ; to elect to membership ; to suspend, expel or disfranchise members ; to make laws for the government of the society ; and was also authorized to issue letters testimonial, under the seal of the society, to such as were found skilled, to the approbation of the examiners, as medical practitioners. A penalty of one hundred pounds ($500) was fixed upon the society and its officers if they should obstinately refuse to examine anybody who presented himself for examination. I believe, sir, that they are now bound to examine anybody, whether a graduate of a college or not, and always have been. It had not occurred to the legislature of Massachusetts at that time that a man was not entitled to practise a profession in which he was skilled unless he had a diploma. It recognized the fact that a quack may exist under the protection of a diploma as well as without it.

The society was organized in June, 1782.

In 1788 it was required to prescribe such a course of medical and surgical instruction, and such qualifications, as they should judge requisite for candidates for the practice of physic or surgery, and to cause the same to be published annually in one or more newspapers in each of four medical districts provided for in the State. (Laws of Mass., vol. III., pp. 140–145.) Here you see a standard for qualification was fixed, and it was a public standard. The Massachusetts Medical Society was the authority to fix the standard and they were required to make the standard known to the people, and every person licensed was required to pay such fees as should be established by the society for examination and license.

In 1802 the examiners or censors of the society were required to examine all who should offer themselves to be approved as practising physicians or surgeons, who had received such an education as was, or might be, from time to time, prescribed by the regulations of the society. An applicant need not necessarily be a graduate of any college, but anybody who came up to the published standard was entitled to examination and to be licensed, if found qualified. And they were required to give every candidate whom they should approve a license to practise physic or surgery, or both. (Laws of Mass., vol. III., pp. 140–145.)

In 1803 it was provided that the members of the Massachusetts Medical Society should not be enrolled in the militia. (Laws of Mass., vol. III., pp. 140–145.)

Then came, in 1817, Mr Chairman, "An Act to Regulate the Practice of Physic and Surgery." This was the first specific act to regulate the practice of physic and surgery in

Massachusetts. It provided that the Massachusetts Medical Society should appoint examiners in each county, who should examine all applicants who had pursued the course of study required by the society, and give licenses to such as were found qualified according to that standard, and also provided that every person licensed by the society to practise should file a copy of his license with the town clerk of the town where he practised. (Laws of 1817, chap. 131.)

It was also further provided by an act in 1818, that any person who had been admitted to the practice of physic or surgery out of the Commonwealth, and had come into it to pursue the practice of the same, might present himself to either of the boards of examiners in the various districts as a candidate for examination, and if they were satisfied that the candidate had received an education agreeably to the regulations provided by the society, — that is, the course of study which was published by the society and had been duly examined and approved by some competent authority, — they might license him to practise physic or surgery, or both, without subjecting him to a new examination. (Laws of 1818, chap. 113.)

Then, in 1819, came a most remarkable act. It was entitled "An Act in Addition to an Act Regulating the Practice of Physic and Surgery." It provided that "No person entering into the practice of physic and surgery after the first day of July, 1819, shall be entitled to the benefit of law for the recovery of any debt or fee for his professional services, unless he shall, previously to rendering those services, have been licensed by the officers of the Massachusetts Medical Society, or shall be graduated a Doctor of Medicine in Harvard University. (Laws of 1819, chap. 113.)

The provision prohibiting anybody but a member of the Massachusetts Medical Society or a graduate of Harvard University from maintaining an action to recover compensation for medical or surgical services was repealed in the revision of the statutes in 1836. The other provisions which I have referred to were incorporated in the provisions of the statutes in 1836, and are found in chapter 22 of the Revised Statutes, entitled " Regulations Concerning the Practice of

Physic and Surgery." This chapter also contains certain other provisions which had been enacted from time to time concerning anatomical science, providing with regard to the use of human dead bodies for dissection and other scientific purposes; and this chapter stood unrepealed and substantially unchanged until 1859, when it was reported by the commissioners for the revision of the statutes as chapter 27 of the Commissioners' Report. This report was submitted by the legislature, at its May session, to a joint special committee of 11 on the part of the Senate, and 28 on the part of the House, together with the President of the Senate and the Speaker of the House. This committee was divided into eight sub-committees, to whom different parts of the Commissioners' Report were referred for examination. Chapter 22 of the Revised Statutes, — that is to say, chapter 27 of the Commissioners' Report, — was referred to a committee composed of six members. The Hon. Increase Sumner of Great Barrington was chairman, and Charles Hale of Boston, subsequently Speaker, was also a member.

On the 16th of May, the general committee instructed this special committee, by special order, to inquire into the expediency of omitting all that part of the chapter relating to the Massachusetts Medical Society, and to the regulation of the practice of medicine; and on the 21st of May they reported to the general committee amendments, striking out every section, and every line and every word in that chapter which gave to the Massachusetts Medical Society any power to examine or license physicians or surgeons, or to prescribe a course of study and qualifications for physicians and surgeons. The general committee adopted these proposed amendments, with the addition of a change of title of the act, from "Regulations Concerning the Practice of Physic and Surgery," to "Of the Promotion of Anatomical Science." And that chapter now stands, with the same title, "Of the Promotion of Anatomical Science," as chapter 81 of the Public Statutes.

All these amendments were adopted by the legislature, and chapter 22 of the Revised Statutes, being chapter 27 of the Commissioners' Report, was enacted as chapter 27 of the

General Statutes, Dec. 28, 1859. A comparison of these chapters and the amendments will show that the legislature then deliberately took out of the law of the Commonwealth every provision for the regulation of the practice of medicine or surgery, or for the examination and qualification of physicians or surgeons. This was not done hastily, Mr. Chairman, for the Commissioners' Report was made on the 15th of December, 1858, and submitted to the legislature in January, 1859. The committee to whom it was referred commenced its work on May 3, 1859, and continued their sessions until Sept. 6, 1859, during a recess of the legislature, and reported to an extra session of the legislature on the 7th of September, 1859, and the General Statutes were enacted on the 28th of December in that year. The matter was thus, as you see, under consideration more than a year.

Nor did this action of the legislature pass unchallenged and undisputed by the Massachusetts Medical Society. The report of the councillors of that society for 1859 shows, that on May 25 they appointed a committee and instructed them to " look after the interests of the society in the legislature, and authorized them to take such measures to protect those interests as they might deem expedient." And yet, in spite of this watchful care of the Massachusetts Medical Society over their rights and privileges, the legislature, without dissent, took every provision for the regulation of the practice of physic and surgery out of the statute law of the Commonwealth, and we have lived without it ever since. (Applause.)

Now, gentlemen, it is sometimes wise to see what kind of men approved legislation. And if you will look to the record, you will find that among the members of the committee who reported this amendment, by which the State went out of the business of supervising the practice of medicine, were the Hon. Increase Sumner of Great Barrington, the Hon. George M Brooks of Concord, afterwards an able member of Congress, and now and for many years the Judge of Probate in Middlesex County, the Hon. Benjamin F. Butler of Lowell, the Hon. Mellen Chamberlain of Chelsea, now the Librarian of the Public Library of Boston, and for

many years Chief Justice of the Municipal Court of Boston,
the Hon. Caleb Cushing of Newburyport, the Hon. Charles
Hale of Boston, the Hon. Amasa Norcross of Fitchburg, the
Hon. Tappan Wentworth of Lowell, the Hon. George M.
Stearns of Chicopee, and the Hon. Thomas H. Russell of
Boston, now the chairman of the Board of Railroad Commissioners. These men were all able and experienced legislators. They did not act hastily or secretly. They acted
deliberately and in the open light of public discussion. The
whole thing was under consideration and discussion for
months. The parties who were most interested in preserv-
ing these statutory provisions took action upon the subject;
and the legislature, as I said before, deliberately took these
laws from the statute books. Do you ask why?

The answer seems to me obvious. The legislature found
that the great power to regulate the practice of medicine,
though in the hands of the wise and able and trained members of the Massachusetts Medical Society, could not be and
had not been exercised, even by them, to the satisfaction of
the people of the Commonwealth. They found that it was
impossible to regulate the practice of an art in which there
is no standard, in which the most distinguished members of
the profession admit that there is no standard, and differ
and quarrel among themselves all the time as to what is best
and right. And for this reason the legislature of Massachusetts wisely said : Let this thing stand upon its own merits;
the people of Massachusetts are educated and intelligent
enough to know what they want (applause) ; we will abandon the system of paternal government, which provides
doctors and nurses and pap for the people under the guise
of protection. And they did abandon it (applause) ; and
we have lived twenty-five years in this Commonwealth, gentlemen, without any statute law whatever upon this subject,
and I represent people who believe that we can live without
any a little longer. (Applause.)

We have not lived during this twenty-five years without
such a law because nobody has asked for it; for there have
been, during this time, repeated attempts by the medical
fraternity, — most of them, I believe, coming from the same

source from which this petition comes,— to have the practice of physic and surgery regulated. One was made in 1877. I hold the bill then asked for in my hand, and I shall be happy to furnish it to the committee if you desire to examine it; it may aid you somewhat. Its provisions are of the same general character as the bill now asked for. I have no doubt it was drawn with great care; I have no doubt the gentlemen who presented it believed it ought to be enacted. They had a very full hearing upon it before the Judiciary Committee That Judiciary Committee was composed of the Hon. Charles Theodore Russell of Cambridge, Mr. Bowman of Middlesex, since member of Congress, Judge White of Plymouth, Mr. Kellogg of Berkshire, and Mr. Coffin of Middlesex, — probably as able a Judiciary Committee as the Senate of Massachusetts has known for fifty years. That committee reported unanimously on the twenty-third day of March, 1877, that the bill ought not to pass. (Applause).

The next year they were up here again, and were sent to the Committee on Water Supply and Drainage (laughter); just why, I don't know, and I have not been able to find anything in the record that would tell. But there it was; and the proposition then took two forms. One was a general bill to regulate the practice of medicine and surgery in the State of Massachusetts; the other was a bill to regulate the practice of medicine and pharmacy in the city of Boston. And those bills contained the provision,— which many medical gentlemen think ought to be in the one asked for this year, — that there should be a fixed representation upon the board of examiners from each of the three medical societies in the Commonwealth. The fate of those bills was this: The bill to regulate the practice of medicine and pharmacy in the city of Boston was reported by a minority of the committee, consisting of Mr. Reed, Mr. Cornish and Mr. Martin. That bill went into the House, and I believe they didn't get votes enough to call the yeas and nays on it. The bill to regulate the practice of medicine and surgery in the State of Massachusetts was reported by the entire committee as inexpedient, so that didn't get any votes. (Applause).

In 1880 they came again, that time under a new bonnet,

— it is sometimes a new bonnet, but it is always the old
face. Then it was under the bonnet of the Social Science
Association, — and then the applicants employed able and
learned counsel. The gentleman who now presides with
such ability in the branch of the legislature in which you,
Mr. Chairman, sit, was counsel for the petitioners; and he
cut the bill down so small that he thought it would go. I
will submit that bill to you, if you would like it; I won't
stop to read it. The essence of this bill was that nobody
should be allowed to practice medicine or use the title of
doctor, or doctor of medicine, in Massachusetts, unless he
had received the degree of doctor of medicine from some
reputable medical institution empowered by special charter
to grant it. That year the Committee on Public Health, to
which the matter was referred, adjourned to the Representa-
tives' Hall and sat for days, and heard everybody, and this
subject was probably discussed in its various aspects with
more learning and more ability than is likely to be brought
to the discussion of it again for a great many years. Well,
they got a bill that time. A short bill was reported by the
committee (Senate Document, No. 198, 1880). But it was
rejected by a very large majority in the House.

There has also been some legislation upon the subject of
medical degrees, to which I desire to call your attention.
In 1874 the legislature provided by a general law that
corporations might be created for medical purposes by vol-
untary associations. (Laws 1874, chap. 375, sect. 2, now
Public Statutes, chap. 115, sect. 2.) Under that act one
or more medical schools or colleges were incorporated in
Massachusetts. And these colleges assumed, as they had
a right to do, to confer degrees. The Massachusetts Medical Society, and its advisers, came to the legislature in 1883,
and said: "We want that provision of the law which
authorizes corporations to be formed for medical instruction
repealed." They got the matter referred to the Committee
on Education, and the Committee on Education reported a
bill, striking the word "medical" out of section 2 of
chapter 115 of the Public Statutes. (House Document, No.
159, 1883.) This would have prevented any corporation

being formed under the general laws for the purpose of medical education; not a very good way to promote medical knowledge and education, I submit. That bill went into the legislature, and there it was rejected, and an act was substituted providing that no corporation organized for medical purposes under the provisions of chapter 115 of the Public Statues should confer degrees, or issue diplomas or certificates, conferring, or purporting to confer, degrees, unless specially authorized by the legislature so to do, with a penalty of $500 in case of violation of the act. (Laws, 1883, chap. 268). That is now the law, and to-day, with the exception of the Harvard Medical School of Harvard University, and the Berkshire School, which I think is under Williams College, and two or three others, and the College of Physicians and Surgeons, in Boston, which has a special authority to confer degrees, but which I believe the Massachusetts Medical Society refuses to recognize, there are no medical schools or colleges in Massachusetts that can confer degrees. So you see the limited number of students in Massachusetts medical schools who could obtain degrees that would entitle them to examination under the proposed legislation.

In 1882 the Massachusetts Dental Society, a sort of an auxiliary of the Massachusetts Medical Society, obtained the passage of a bill " to regulate the practice of dentistry," for the purpose, as they claimed, of keeping the profession clear of impostors; but that wise and sagacious magistrate, John D. Long, who was then Governor of the Commonwealth, promptly returned it to the Senate with a veto message, in which he said: " If such legislation is required for dentists, it is not easy to see why there should not be similar special legislation concerning cooks, plumbers, apothecaries, and the other businesses which involve life and health;" and, also, that " it would, perhaps, be better worth while to consider the expediency of a general statute to the effect that any person pursuing a business or profession, without sufficient skill therein, shall be punished. Such a statute, in the hands of judge and jury, would never work injustice, and yet would be ample for those exceptional cases of imposition, on the strength of which various special statutes are urged from year to year." I respectfully commend this last suggestion to the careful consideration of this committee.

After this message had been read in the Senate, the question was put "Shall the bill pass, the objections of the Governor to the contrary notwithstanding?" One Senator only voted for the bill, and thirty voted against it.

There has been one other attempt to obtain legislation upon this subject, or upon subjects analogous to this, up to the present time; and that was last year, when a bill was introduced to regulate the sale of patent medicines and proprietary articles. That was sent to the Committee on Public Health, which reported it ought not to pass.

Now, you will find by the record, Mr. Chairman, that none of these applications have been made by the people. They have all been made by gentlemen of the medical profession. They say they have made them for the protection of the people. By what divine right they are authorized to act as protectors of the people of Massachusetts they do not show. (Laughter.) They held the control of the matter for more than half a century, and the people took it away from them. For twenty-five years the people have kept it away from them, and I believe they will continue to do so for an hundred years to come. (Applause.) The people have never asked any change, and they do not ask it now. There was, however, until this winter, to my mind, a very sound reason why there should be legislation upon this subject. And it is found in the statement contained in the preamble of the petition of the Social Science Association in 1880, that " by the laws of this State death caused by culpable and reckless ignorance of duty is not considered manslaughter by the courts in regard to physicians, although it is held to be manslaughter in the case of those following other callings; so that ignorant and self-styled physicians are not restrained by fear of the law from recklessly trifling with the lives of the citizens of this State." And that was the fact; such was the law at that time. And yet, in spite of that fact, the legislature refused to regulate the practice. The learned gentleman who represented the petitioners at that time, the present President of the Senate, said, — I quote from his printed argument, — " In this condition of things, we ask you to interfere." That was his main, almost his only, argument. He said : " The Supreme Court of Massachusetts, in Commonwealth *v.* Thompson (6 Mass. Reports, 134), which was decided in 1809, and which every doctor knows about, and most people have heard of, held that a man who practised medicine, — who attempted to cure, — if he acted honestly, although he was grossly negligent, although he was presumptuous, could not be convicted of manslaughter, or of assault, or any crime, and, therefore, he said there ought to be legislation to regulate it ; that if physicians were protected under the law from the consequences of the same things which, if done by others, would send them to State prison, then the practice of physic should be regulated. And I thought so too. But such is not the law of Massachusetts to-day. That old decision of the court was not conceived by the profession to be sound ; and, in Worcester County, a man by the name of Pierce was indicted at the May term of the Superior Criminal Court, in 1884, for manslaughter, in causing the death of Mrs. Mary A. Bemis, in the application of kerosene oil, with her consent, by covering the deceased with flannel saturated with oil, for two or three days, in consequence of which she died. On the trial, before His Honor Judge Pitman, the counsel for Pierce contended that under the decision of Commonwealth *v.* Thompson, to which I have referred, the killing, to constitute manslaughter, must have been the consequence of some unlawful act, and what he had done was not unlawful, because it was done as a physician in the attempt to heal the woman. They asked the court to rule that, " There is no law which prohibits any man from prescribing for a sick man, with his consent, if he honestly intends to cure by his prescription. A patient has a right to employ whom he pleases to treat him, and acceptance of the employment by one who honestly believes he is able, and honestly intends to cure, is not a felonious act, however ignorant of medicine he may be in fact." But the court, against the defendant's objection, ruled as follows : " It is not necessary to show an evil intent ; if, by gross and reckless negligence, the defendant caused the death, he is guilty of culpable homicide." Upon this ruling, Pierce was found guilty by the jury and convicted. The case went to the Supreme Court on exceptions to this ruling, and I have here the opinion of the court, in which they sustain the ruling of Judge Pitman ; and Pierce is now serving a sentence of six years in the State prison for manslaughter.

Thus you see that the law in Massachusetts is now that every man or woman has a right to practise the healing art, but practises it at his or her peril. If he is ignorant or negligent, he is liable in damages civilly. The rule which covers the liability of a physician is not different from that which covers the liability of a farrier who shoes a horse, or a man who assumes to do anything in a particular calling. A man who assumes to do a particular thing for you, Mr. Chairman, because that is his profession, impliedly says to you, " I have sufficient skill and ability to do it." A man who assumes to minister to you in sickness, impliedly says to you, " I know enough of the art to minister to you wisely and skilfully and well ; I am a physician ; I am learned enough to treat the disease which I assume to treat." Not necessarily to treat every disease, but the disease he assumes to treat. The man who holds himself out as being competent to treat a fever does not necessarily say, " I am competent to amputate a leg, or to perform the operation of ovariotomy." The law is very plain and simple. The man who says, " I can treat you for a fever, or for the ague," impliedly contracts for skill and learning sufficient to do that and nothing else, and the law ought not to require anything else of him. Under the proposed bill, however, he must not only have knowledge to treat a fever, but he must be a surgeon and a dentist, and the man who assumes to fill teeth must be a physician and a surgeon. The examination for admission to practice is made the same for dentists, surgeons and physicians. The present law is clear and ample. A man or woman who assumes to practise the healing art, impliedly contracts that he or she has sufficient skill and knowledge to do the thing which they assume to do, to cure the disease which they assume to treat, and no other. And if he or she does not have it, they are liable in damages for all the consequences that result from the lack of knowledge and skill. If he or she is grossly or presumptuously ignorant and negligent, and a person is thereby killed or injured, he or she is liable for manslaughter or for an assault. The same principle that made Pierce liable for manslaughter because Mrs. Bemis died, would have made him liable for an assault, if she had lived and been a cripple. Every man, woman or child in Massachusetts who assumes to practise medicine, who assumes to heal others, does so at his or her peril absolutely. Now, I submit, that is all the law we need. (Applause.) We have got on under that law — under a law much less stringent than that until this year — well enough for twenty-five years. Now you are asked by the Massachusetts Medical Society to change it.

Nobody asks for it but the doctors. We have had nineteen doctors here in favor of it, and one was a horse doctor. They are all excellent men, all gentlemen worthy of respect, and they ought to be heard, and have been heard fully. They had a right to come here to get such legislation as they think the Commonwealth needs, or their own interests require. Only a part of them, however, were frank enough to say that what they were after was protection. The medical gentleman who came up from Plymouth County said, "We think we ought to be protected against these quacks. Why! there are six of them down in my county," he says; "all having a large practice." (Laughter.) And, said he, "some of them cannot read nor write." Well, what if they can't, if they cure diseases? — if they do what they assume to do? If a man comes to cure me of a disease, — of a fever or the ague, — and he cures me, I don't care whether he can read the New Testament in Greek, as the Rev. Dr. Warren says every man who claims to be liberally educated ought to be able to do, or whether he can write his name. If he does not cure me, if he is negligent, if he has not the skill which he assumes to have, why then he is liable to me in damages. If he is grossly and wilfully and presumptuously ignorant and negligent and he injures me, he is liable criminally. I need no other protection. The people need no other protection. My friend, Mr. Gargan, said to Dr. Abbott, as you remember, "How is it about the people being unanimous for this, when there is such a large practice for all these quacks?" "Oh!" he said, "I didn't say the people were unanimous for it; I said the doctors were." (Laughter.)

We have had three clergymen here, presumably at the request of the doctors. The first was the Rev. Dr. Warren, who is the president of Boston University, and who has, of course, every year a fair crop of new-fledged doctors of medicine to provide places for; and he would be very glad that nobody should be allowed to practise the healing art except those who had diplomas. He would be very glad, I have no doubt, to have as narrow a circle from which to draw doctors as possible, and then his graduates would stand a better chance. But I do not think the Doctor was actuated by that motive, or knew that he was. Sometimes, however, men are actuated by motives of which they are not really conscious. I think the Doctor felt there ought to be some legislation. But about all he said was he wanted to have some sign by which people could tell whether a man was a doctor or not. Well, I don't object, and I don't know that anybody objects, to a law, if it is necessary and discreet, compelling every doctor to put on his sign the name of the college from which he graduated; and if he did not graduate from any college to put that fact on his sign too. (Laughter.) My knowledge of physicians has been somewhat extensive, and I do not believe that the fact that a man graduated from the Harvard Medical School, engraved upon his door-plate, would drive away a great many patients. At any rate people might choose, and I don't know anybody who would object to that. It is precisely this liberty of choice which ought to be preserved, and which the proposed bill takes away.

Then comes the Right Rev. Dr. Byrnes, and I could not but remember, when he was talking, the historical fact that the great religious denomination of which he is an honored member, and which I believe does a great deal of good to-day, has always claimed the right to regulate men's morals by law, and once practically claimed the right to regulate the practice of medicine also, and ordained that any woman who practised medicine without its sanction should be deemed to be a witch. I take it the people of Massachusetts will not profit by going to that school for instruction. (Applause.) But even Dr. Byrnes did not tell you he approved the proposed bill.

Then we had the Rev. Dr. Webb, a gentleman widely known, of great learning and of most excellent intentions. But he, too, belongs to the old red sandstone age. (Laughter.) It is within the past twelve months, I think, — certainly within two years, — that he was opposed to settling one of the most able and eloquent ministers of his denomination as pastor in the Old South Church of Boston because he could not swallow quite all the ultra dogmas of the extreme Calvinistic creed. (Laughter.) Knowing this, I was not surprised when Dr. Webb told you that he thought the State ought to guarantee sound education and competency in teachers of morals and practitioners of medicine. And I agree that if it is bound to do the one it is bound to do the other. (Applause.)

Now, Mr. Chairman and gentlemen, you have had no evidence in favor of this petition. No fact has been given to you. No one of these gentlemen, so competent, so trained, so well fitted to instruct you, has given you any facts. They have dosed you with their opinions, which you probably knew before; but they have given you no facts. They have formulated no charges against anybody. I could not but think, sir, yesterday, when Judge Ladd of Cambridge, who is known and respected of all men in the community where he has lived for more than half a century, filling an important judicial office with honesty and fairness and dignity, was giving you, specifically, case after case to show that his view of the healing art was correct, — a view, by the way, in which I cannot personally agree, — how different the clear, the careful, the accurate, specific statements that he made to you were from the rhetorical efforts of the gentlemen in behalf of the petitioners. (Applause.)

Not a non-professional man has said a word in favor of any legislation. And yet this hearing is so widely known and excites such interest in the public mind that this large room is not sufficient to accommodate those who desire to come. The petitioners say that quackery is so rampant in the Commonwealth, and the evils resulting from the fact that you have no law regulating the practice of medicine are so great, that the people are crying out for the proposed legislation! And yet not a man, woman or child, outside of the three doctors of divinity and the nineteen doctors of medicine, — seventeen of them, I believe, members of the Massachusetts Medical Society, — has come here to raise a voice in favor of such legislation. I know the legislation is not called for by the people, and I believe that it is unwise and unnecessary.

There is no standard by which you can regulate the practice of medicine. That is the root of this matter. There is no standard in the different schools. Do you not find, in every country town, gentlemen of the same school quarrelling over the practice of their profession, oftentimes in as unseemly a way as the medical gentlemen have quarrelled before you? There are mistakes in all the schools. I have no doubt there is good in all the schools. I am free to say that if any legislation was to be had, from my standpoint it would be legislation which made the Massachusetts Medical Society the sole judge, because I belong to that school in medicine as much as I belong to any, and if I were to be doctored to death I should prefer to be doctored to death by a man of the old school rather than of the new. (Laughter.) But I do not believe it is any more just or right to exclude my friend Judge Ladd, who wants to be doctored by a magnetic healer, or by a Christian scientist, or by somebody who does not profess to practise medicine according to any of the recognized schools, from exercising his choice, than it would be to debar me from the right to be doctored to death by my friend Dr. Marcy, if I chose to employ him, as very likely I should. (Laughter.)

Why, they differ in therapeutics, as we all know. They differ in *Materia Medica*, as we all know. They differ even in pathology and anatomy,— at least, they quarrel over it. Within six months I have had a case in this city, where I had upon the one side three of the ablest pathologists of the so-called regular school as witnesses in behalf of my client, and on the other side were three of the leading surgeons of the homœopathic school in Massachusetts, and upon precisely the same facts, upon precisely the same autopsy, at which they were all present, they came to diametrically opposite results, and disputed over it just as badly as the homœopaths and the allopaths always dispute. You find an illustration of this in all expert testimony. I have seen — everybody who is familiar with the courts has seen — doctors, able men, learned men, honest men, who believed it, and who had opportunity to inform themselves, come into court and testify that the plaintiff would never recover from certain injuries; and yet I have seen that same plaintiff, under the curative power of a verdict, take up his bed and walk, and go about his business in six months afterwards. (Laughter.) I know of a case in my practice where five of the ablest surgeons in Massachusetts, on my side of the case, testified that a man, — who was brought into court upon his bed, who said he could not walk, who said he could not stand or use his hands, — could get up if he only tried, and would get up as soon as the case was decided, and get well and go about his business, and they all believed it; and if they did not know, as I argued to the jury, there was no one in Massachusetts that did know. And yet that man, who obtained a very large verdict two years ago, is still in substantially the same condition that he was then. Talk about a standard in medicine ! I want no better evidence that there is no standard than this hearing has given us by the unseemly contests of the doctors before you.

It may be said to be presumptuous, perhaps, for me to say there is no standard, though I believe myself that Voltaire was right when he said that "the art of medicine consists in amusing the patient, while Nature cures the disease." (Laughter.) But I desire to call your attention to the opinions of a few of the ablest members of the medical profession upon this subject. Dr. Chapman, Professor of the Practice

of Physic in the University of Philadelphia says : " Consult-
ing the records of our science, we cannot help being dis-
gusted with the multitude of hypotheses obtruded upon us at
different times. Nowhere is the imagination displayed to a
greater extent ; and perhaps so ample an exhibition of human
invention might gratify our vanity, if it were not more than
compensated by the humiliating view of so much absurdity,
contradiction and falsehood. To harmonize the contrarieties
of medical doctrines is, indeed, a task as impracticable as to
arrange the fleeting vapors around us." Dr. Abercrombie,
Fellow of the Royal Society of England, and of the Royal
College of Physicians in Edinburgh, says : " Medicine has
been called by philosophers the art of conjecturing, the science of guessing." Sir John Forbes, Fellow of the Royal
College of Physicians, London, physician of the Queen's
household, etc., says : " No systematic or theoretical classifi-
cation of diseases or therapeutic agents ever yet promul-
gated is true, or anything like the truth, and none can be
adopted as a safe guidance in practice." Dr. James Johnson
of London, Surgeon Extraordinary to the King, etc., said :
" I declare my conscientious opinion, founded on long observation and reflection, that if there was not a single physician, surgeon, apothecary, man midwife, chemist, druggist
or drug on the face of the earth there would be less sickness
and less mortality than now obtains." Coming nearer home,
Dr. Jacob Bigelow, a former President of the Massachusetts
Medical Society, in his " Expositions of Rational Medicine,"
says : " I sincerely believe that the unbiased opinion of most
medical men of sound judgment and long experience is, that
the amount of death and disaster in the world would be less
than it now is, if all disease were left to itself." Sir William
Hamilton, in his " Discussions on Philosophy," p. 638,— an
authority that I know my medical friends will respect, —
says : " The history of medicine, on the one hand, is nothing
less than a history of variations ; and on the other, only a
still more marvellous history of how every successive varia-
tion has by medical bodies been furiously denounced, and
then bigotedly adopted." If you will turn to Thatcher's History of Medicine in America, pp. 21, 22, you will find that

when Dr. Boylston, in 1721, introduced vaccination into Boston, "most of the medical faculty were its active and violent opposers."

Dr. Oliver Wendell Holmes, formerly Professor of Anatomy in the Medical School of Harvard University, in his "Border Lines of Knowledge," p. 70, says : "The disgrace of medicine has been that colossal system of self-deception, in obedience to which mines have been emptied of their cankering minerals, the entrails of animals taxed for their impurities, the poison-bags of reptiles drained of their venom, and all the inconceivable abominations thus obtained thrust down the throats of human beings suffering from some fault of organization, nourishment or vital stimulation."

Bichat (the great French pathologist), in his "General Anatomy," vol. I., p. 17, says : "Medicine is an incoherent assemblage of incoherent ideas, and is perhaps of all the physiological sciences that which best shows the caprice of the human mind. What did I say? It is not a science for a methodical mind. It is a shapeless assemblage of inaccurate ideas, of observations often puerile, and of formulæ as fantastically conceived as they are tediously arranged."

The late Sir Henry Holland, one of the most eminent physicians in Europe, in his "Recollections of Past Life," p. 88, says : "Actual experience, with a sense of responsibility attached to it, is the sole school in which to make a good physician. One of the most learned men I ever knew in the literature of medicine, as well as in physical science, was one of the worst practitioners, borrowing his diagnosis from books, and not from that happier faculty, *almost an instinct, a spiritual gift, which enables some men to interpret and act upon signs which no book can describe.*"

Dr. L. M. Whiting, in a dissertation delivered at an annual commencement in Pittsfield, Mass., and recorded in the Boston Medical and Surgical Journal, vol. 14, p. 183, says : "The very principles upon which most of what are called the theories involving medical questions have been based were never *established*. They are, and always were, false ; and consequently the superstructures built upon them were the baseless fabric of a vision — transient in their existence —

passing away upon the introduction of new doctrines and hypotheses like dew before the morning sun. Speculation has been the garb in which medicine has been arrayed, from the remote period when it was rocked in the cradle of its infancy by the Egyptian priesthood, down to the present day; system after system has arisen, flourished, fallen and been forgotten, in rapid and melancholy succession, until the whole field is strewed with the disjointed materials in a perfect chaos, and amongst the rubbish the philosophic mind may search for ages without being able to glean from it *hardly one solitary well-established fact.*"

It is not strange that Dr. Benjamin Waterhouse, who for twenty years was a professor in the Medical School of Harvard University, at the close of his time said: "I am sick of learned quackery." The great German physician Boerhaave ordered in his will, I believe, that all his library should be burned, except one book, which he said contained the whole art of medicine. After his death, I believe they did not burn the whole library, but they looked for that one book with great anxiety. Its pages were all found to be blank but one, and upon that was written, "Bowels open, head cold and feet warm, and physicians will get poor." Dr. Holmes stated once, I believe, in an address to the Massachusetts Medical Society, that he thought it would be better for mankind if all the medicines were poured into the sea, although he thought it would be hard on the fishes. (Laughter.) Perhaps this was one of the genial jokes of the autocrat of the breakfast-table. He did say, on this subject, however, the following, which is not in the nature of a joke, but what he undoubtedly thought and taught. In his essay, read before the Massachusetts Medical Society, at the annual meeting May 30th, 1860, he said: "A glance at the prevalent modes of treatment of any two successive generations, will show that there is a changeable, as well as a permanent, element in the art of healing; not merely changeable as diseases vary, or as new remedies are introduced, but changeable by the going out of fashion of special remedies. The truth is that medicine, professedly founded on observation, is as sensitive to outside influences, political, philosophical, imaginative, as is the barometer to the changes of atmospheric density."

You all remember Lord Macaulay's vivid account of the death of Charles II., when "the fourteen doctors who deliberated on the king's case contradicted each other and themselves. Some of them thought his fit was epileptic, and that he should be suffered to have his doze out. The majority pronounced him apoplectic and tortured him like an Indian at the stake. It was then determined to call his complaint a fever and to administer doses of bark." I suppose that means quinine. "Several of the prescriptions have been preserved. One of them is signed by fourteen doctors. The patient was bled freely. Hot iron was applied to his head. A loathsome volatile salt, extracted from human skulls, was forced into his mouth." (Macaulay's Hist. England, vol. 2, pp. 6, 15.) No wonder the poor king apologized for being such an unconscionable time dying! And yet, all these fourteen physicians were men licensed under a system precisely such as the people of Massachusetts destroyed in 1860, and as the Massachusetts Medical Society now asks you to re-establish. (Applause and laughter.) The Act of 14–15 Henry VIII. gave to the College of Physicians, corresponding exactly to the Massachusetts Medical Society, the whole power of examination and license of physicians for England; so that, as the preamble provided, the practice of the healing art should be confined to "those persons that be profound, sad and discreet, and deeply studied in physic." (Knight's Hist. England, vol. 2, p. 497.)

But, it is said, you inspect fish, you inspect oil, you inspect gas, you license lawyers; why should you not inspect physicians and license them? I have a list from the statutes, which I will hand to the committee, embracing every case in which inspection is called for of any article sold in Massachusetts. It includes petroleum, and fish, and hops, and milk, and sperm oils, and intoxicating liquors, and hoops and staves, and lime, and vinegar, etc.; and in every one of these cases, where the standard is not one that everybody would recognize, — as, for instance, diseased meat, or decayed fruit, where you need no standard to be established by law or by a medical examination, for everybody understands what decayed fruit is and what is diseased meat, — in every case where there is any standard necessary to be defined, the statute fixes it.

The statute which provides for the inspection of fish, fixes definitely the standard for such inspection. (Public Statutes, chapter 56, sections 25, 26, 32, 37.) The statute which regulates the sale of milk provides that milk shall be deemed to be adulterated which contains more than eighty-seven per cent. of watery fluid, or less than thirteen per cent. of milk solids, and thus establishes an absolute standard for the guidance of dealers. (Public Statutes, chapter 57, section 9.) The statute for the inspection of illuminating gas and gas meters fixes a unit of measure and an absolute standard of quality. (Public Statutes, chapter 61, sections 8, 14.) The statute regulating the sale of naphtha and illuminating oils fixes the standard of quality by express and specific terms, and even provides that the test shall be made by a particular kind of instrument for that purpose. (Public Statutes, chapter 102, sections 69, 70.) The statute which regulates the sale of intoxicating liquors provides specifically what liquors shall be deemed intoxicating within the law. (Public Statutes, chapter 100, section 27.) The law regulating the inspection and sale of sperm oils provides that the test shall be Harris' oleometer. (Public Statutes, chapter 59, section 5.) The statutes regulating the sale of hops, lime, hoops and staves, vinegar and lumber, all prescribe certain and definite standards of quality in express terms. (Public Statutes, chapter 56, sections 31, 32; chapter 60, sections 49, 70; chapter 63, sections 8 to 16 inclusive.)

And in the building laws, which are talked about, there is a standard fixed by the law, and there are two pages of the Public Statutes filled with the most exact and complete description of the kind of lumber that shall constitute the various qualities recognized to be sold under the law. (Laughter.)

And there is a standard for the qualification of lawyers.

Turn to chapter 159 of the Public Statutes, sections 34 to 41 inclusive, and you will find the regulations for admission to the practice of the law. There is a very general impression in the community that a man cannot practise law without being examined and licensed and admitted to the bar; but it is not correct. There is nothing to-day to prevent our friend Dr. Marcy from going down on State Street and hiring an office and putting out his sign and styling himself an attorney-at-law, and doing all the law business for anybody that he can get to do. If he is not an attorney-at-law, and he tells a man falsely he is, he is liable precisely as anybody else is liable for false pretences; but there is no statute law specifically prohibiting him from doing such business. A man may open an office, he may draw papers, he may give advice, he may do all kinds of law business, except going into court and trying cases, generally as an officer of the court, as a part of the machinery of the courts, without leave or license of anybody. It is his right as much as it is to make boots and shoes or sell goods.

Now, let us see how it is when he goes into court. If a man wants to be an attorney, an officer of the court, admitted to do general business and to try causes generally in court, without nomination by his client in each case, he must be admitted to the bar. He must take an oath fully set forth and prescribed by the statute. But, mark you, there is a standard by which a lawyer can be examined. If the question is asked, What is the law on such a subject? we turn to the statute or to the decided cases and find it. What is the law in regard to the punishment of a physician who is ignorant and presumptuously and wilfully negligent in the treatment of a patient, whereby the patient is either injured or dies? We turn to the opinion of the Supreme Court in Commonwealth *v.* Pierce, and find what the law is. There is a standard for qualification for admission to the bar, and a standard by which to examine candidates, — the statute law of the Commonwealth and the 136 volumes of reported decisions, — and you know when the applicant makes a correct answer to questions. Not so in medicine. Ask what is necessary to constitute an estate of inheritance in Massachusetts, and there is but one possible answer. Ask what is the proper treatment for a fever, and there are more answers than there are different schools of medicine.

But, leaving that, section 40 of chapter 159, Public Statutes, provides that parties may manage, prosecute or defend their own suits personally. Well, I believe this bill does leave people the right to take drugs themselves. (Laughter.) Section 41 provides that " any person of good moral character, unless he has been removed from practice as an attorney, under section 39, by the court, may manage, prosecute or defend a suit, if he is specially authorized by the party for whom he appears, in writing or by personal nomination in open court." That is to say, I can go down to the court, and I can say I want my friend Dr. Wilson to try a case for me, and the court are bound to hear him for me. I need not put anything in writing; I can simply say, " Dr. Wilson is my attorney," and the court are bound to hear him. It is my constitutional and legal right to be heard by him, or by any reputable person, learned or unlearned, with a diploma or without a diploma ; and that is all we want to preserve for the people as against the physicians. All we want to preserve is the right of every man or woman of full age and sound mind in Massachusetts to have such person minister to them in disease or sickness as they wish. (Applause.) And when the medical profession say that doctors should be examined and licensed, because a man who becomes an officer of the court is examined and licensed by the court, I say : Put into any bill that they may. bring here a provision that any person may have the same right with regard to his choice of his physician or his surgeon that he has to-day with regard to his lawyer, and I am content. (Applause.) But they don't mean it, and they won't do it.

Dr. Marcy. Yes, we will.

Mr. Benton. Then, why don't you put it in your bill; year after year such an amendment has been proposed, and it has always been rejected by your society.

Now, Mr. Chairman, I am taking a good deal more time than I meant to take. I think this proposed legislation is going back to the dark ages. It is simply an odious form of the most odious kind of government, a paternal government which regards the subjects of the State as children, to be fed and nursed because they cannot take care of themselves. It was once extended in England to overlooking modes of manufacture and agricultural operations and domestic affairs. It directed farmers at what fairs they should sell their products; it prescribed the quantity of ale to be sold for a penny; it made it penal to sell any pins except those of a certain specified character; and it directed farmers what crops they should raise, and how much. In China this kind of government has regulated the dress; in Austria it has regulated the literature; in Germany it has prevented shoemakers from following their craft until an inspecting jury has certified to their competence, has forbidden a man who had adopted one calling from ever taking up another, and also forbidden any foreign tradesman from settling in a German town without a license. Under this theory the governments of olden times regulated the creeds and the morals of their subjects, and upon this theory of the province of government Sir David Brewster, in an address to the British Association in Edinburgh in 1850, advocated a scheme very much like that which the Rev. Dr. Webb has advocated before you of having " men ordained by the State to the undivided functions of science, an intellectual priesthood, to develop the glorious truths which time and space embosom." That was in 1850, and it was exactly in the line of this theory that a priesthood of physic has always been advocated by certain theoretical medical gentlemen. In the reign of Edward IV. those wearing any gown or mantle not according to specification were fined. In the reign of Charles II. the length of people's boot-toes and the material of their grave clothes were prescribed by statute.

If a government is to enter upon this line of legislation at all, I submit it will be entirely proper that it should deal with the matter of health, and in so doing it ought to re-enact those ancient statutes which protected people's stomachs by restricting the expense of their tables; and, to prevent the injury which undoubtedly arises to a large portion of our population from fashionable late hours, it ought to revive the old Norman custom and fix the time at which people should put out their fires and go to bed. Or, acting upon the opinion of an eminent French statesman, — I believe the law of France has been cited by the petitioners for your guidance, — that it was "proper to watch during the fruit season lest the people eat that which is not ripe," the government should make it unlawful to sell or eat fruit until its quality has been approved by a medical board. And in order to make the care of the State in this example quite complete, sir, it would be well to follow the example of the Danish king, who provided by law how his subjects should scour their floors and polish their furniture.

And you should also certainly provide for the examination and license of nurses as well as physicians, for every one knows that a good nurse is of even more importance in sickness than a good physician. And following the same line of legislation you should certainly regulate the charges of all physicians and surgeons, for if it is the duty of the State to protect its citizens against practitioners who are ignorant, it is equally its duty to protect them against practitioners who are extortionate.

The theory that a government is bound to guarantee to its citizens or subjects that every person who undertakes to practise physic or surgery shall be thoroughly qualified and competent, or, as is stated by a majority of the medical profession who ask for this bill, that the State should interpose between quacks and those who patronize them, is not essentially different from all other govermental interferences with trade. One of the most profound philosophers of the English-speaking race, Herbert Spencer, treats upon this subject as follows : "The invalid is at liberty to buy medicine and advice from whomsoever he pleases ; the licensed practitioner is at liberty to sell these to whomsoever will buy. On no pretext whatever can a barrier be set up between these without the law of equal freedom being broken, and least of all may the government, whose office it is to uphold that law, become a transgressor of it. Health depends upon the fulfilment of numerous conditions." If this legislation is designed for any purpose, it is designed to protect health. "It can be protected only by the fulfilment of those conditious. If, therefore, it is the duty of the State to protect the health of its subjects by licensing physicians, then it is its duty to see that all the conditions of health are fulfilled by them. Shall this duty be consistently discharged? If so, the legislature must enact a national dietary ; prescribe so many meals a day for each individual ; fix the quantities and qualities of food, both for men and women ; state the proportion of fluids, when to be taken and of what kind"— that would be troublesome in Boston ; "specify the amount of exercise and define its character ; describe the clothing to be worn ; determine the hours of sleep, allowing for the difference of age and sex ; and so on, with other particulars necessary to complete a perfect synopsis for the daily guidance of the nation. And to enforce these regulations it must employ a sufficient establishment of well-qualified officers empowered to direct everybody's domestic arrangements." (Social Statics, pp. 407, 408.)

As I have said, Mr. Chairman, the proposed legislation is going back to a system which the people of the Commonwealth tried for many years and then deliberately abandoned. They do not need this legislation ; they do not ask for it. It is in the wrong direction and unnecessary and uncalled for by the people. Now, I want to say only a word or two more about this proposed bill, for I have talked longer than I meant to. I object to this bill, in the first place, because it assumes that a diploma never covers a quack. Take the first section of it : "There shall be established a board of medical examiners, consisting of nine men, appointed by the Governor and Council. They shall be graduates of a legally chartered college or university having the power to confer medical degrees." Why, under that very section, it would be competent for the Governor to appoint anybody who had a diploma and who had practised ten years ; and if you cannot pick out of the sixteen hundred members of the Massachusetts Medical Society,— to say nothing of members of other societies, and graduates of medical colleges who are not members of any societies, — nine quacks who have practised ten years I shall be very much surprised. You cannot get sixteen hundred physicians in one body without having quacks among them, no matter what school they belong to. A diploma does not insure honesty, capacity, knowledge, intelligence and fidelity to the profession. (Applause.) But this bill assumes it as an essential requisite. Again, the bill puts a premium on old quacks. It says that a man who has been a quack in Massachusetts for ten years shall stay, he shall have the approval of the State to stay; not merely stay here at his peril, as he does now, but he shall stay here licensed to practise his nefarious calling under the law. Because, forsooth, a man has been doing wrong ten years, — because he has been acting ignorantly and wilfully for ten years,— he shall have a right to go on for any number of years more; but if he has only done it one year he shall be cut off; if he has done it nine years and eleven months he shall be cut off. It is wrong! It is wrong! If such legislation means anything, — if you are going to regulate the practice of medicine and surgery at all, gentlemen, — create a standard, just as the Massachusetts Medical Society did; a standard that means something and that people can know something about. Ordain arbitrarily that homœopathy is wrong and allopathy is right, or that homœopathy is right and allopathy is wrong, or that eclecticism is right and everything else is wrong. Then, when you have done that, provide that everybody who does not practise according to the standard shall be driven out of business, whether he has been in it one year or fifty.

Again, the bill creates another commission to be added to the numerous commissions with which the Commonwealth is already burdened. It provides for expenses of about $6,000, I think, — $500 apiece to the nine medical examiners, $4,500; $1,500 to the secretary, and expenses as great as the consciences of the secretary of the board and of the auditing officer may be elastic; all to be paid from the State treasury. (Laughter.) We don't want any more expenses of that kind than we are now saddled with.

It then gives a premium to this board to reject people.

It says that an applicant shall pay a fee of twenty dollars, which shall not be returned if a certificate is refused. Now, look at that. Here is a young man who has gone through the Harvard Medical School, or through the Boston University Medical School. He wants to practise his profession. He comes up to be examined and he fails. He is overworked, he is diffident; perhaps he is not quite up in some branch, and he cannot be passed fairly. He fails. He has paid twenty dollars; and I know, sir, and many people here know, that twenty dollars is a great deal of money to a young professional man when he is first struggling into life. He goes back to his studies and in six months comes up for re-examination, and then he must pay twenty dollars more. That is wrong! If this is legislation in the interest of the people, let the people pay the expenses of examination. Do not put it upon the young men who are struggling to come into the honorable profession of medicine. Levy a tax on me and on you, and you, and everybody else in Massachusetts, and pay the expense of protecting the people by a general tax upon the people.

Again, the bill necessarily excludes persons who may do good in the healing art, who are not graduates of any medical school. Dr. Marcy shakes his head, and he ought to know his bill better than I do; but I understand this to be the effect of the bill. In the first place it provides that after this act takes effect, " the following persons and no others shall be permitted to practise medicine, surgery or dentistry : All persons who are graduates of a legally chartered medical or dental college. Every such person shall present his diploma to the said board of medical examiners, and, if the same be found to be genuine, and was issued by such college as is hereinbefore mentioned, etc." Now, I suppose under that, all the leading physicians and surgeons in Boston would be obliged to take their diplomas and go before this board. Imagine such men as Hodges and Cheever and Talbot being obliged to come before this board appointed by the Governor and Council, and say, " Won't you please put on this diploma of mine the evidence that I am competent to practise medicine." (Laughter.)

Then the bill further says that everybody who is not a graduate, but who has practised medicine, surgery or dentistry in this State continuously for the period of ten years prior to the first day of July, 1885, may keep right on practising, but must first make an affidavit of that fact, which shall be received as true, unless the board prove it to be false. That takes care of everybody in Massachusetts who is practising at the present time.

And then the seventh section provides that "after July, 1876, the State Board of Medical Examiners shall examine all applicants for license to practise medicine, surgery or dentistry, in this Commonwealth. Applicants must give satisfactory proof of being twenty-one years of age, of good moral character, and *of having received a diploma from some legally chartered medical college or university.*" Now, does not that make the possession of such a diploma a prerequisite to examination? Clearly it does. Under that act, if you should adopt it, a man who was not a graduate of a legally chartered medical college could not be examined for admission to the practice of medicine in Massachusetts, no matter how much he knew, no matter how good his morals were. Anybody can be examined to be admitted to the practice of law. We have had men who were good physicians, who had no diplomas; we have had men who were good lawyers and good judges, who had no diplomas. The people never yet had any profound conviction of the difference between a good doctor with a diploma, and a good doctor without one; between a good lawyer without a diploma, and a good lawyer with one.

Again, the bill creates a medical tribunal,—and this is the great objection to any legislation of this kind, — it creates an arbitrary medical tribunal, with power to take from men the means by which they get their living. Turn to the last clause of section 8 : "Said Board of Medical Examiners may revoke a license for unprofessional or dishonorable conduct upon a unanimous vote, after giving the accused an opportunity to be heard in defence." Now, the suggestion was made, What is the harm in that, if it is by a unanimous vote? Turn to the last clause of section 13 : " A majority

of the members of said Board of Medical Examiners created by this act, when qualified according to the provisions
of this act,"—I don't know how they are qualified, there is
no provision for qualifying,—"are authorized and empowered to exercise all the powers and perform all the duties
authorized and required by said board, by the provisions of
this act;" the effect of which would be, sir, that five gentlemen could call any member of the medical profession in
Massachusetts before them, and without charges, without
evidence, not for any crime, not for any neglect of duty,
not for any malpractice in the profession, but for anything
which they thought was "unprofessional or dishonorable,"
absolutely, and without appeal or remedy, take away from
that man the power to earn his bread. No such power
ought to be conferred upon any five men or nine men,
or any number of men, no matter whether they act by
a majority vote or a unanimous vote. A man's profession is property as much as houses or lands. And no
man or woman should be deprived of the right to practise the calling by which they gain their bread, without
a fair and open trial conducted under the rules of evidence
and practice established by the law of the land. (Applause.) Why, sir, even a member of the bar can be
removed from his office only upon charges, only upon a
trial in open court, with the right to go to the full court of
the Commonwealth upon all questions of law. He cannot
be removed arbitrarily by any Star Chamber practice like
that proposed by this bill. Under this act — under any act
which will satisfy these medical gentlemen — it is in the
power of a board of medical men, without remedy, without
appeal, to take out of the mouth of any practitioner in the
State the power to earn the bread on which he and his family
live.

> "You take my house when you do take the prop
> That doth sustain my house; you take my life
> When you do take the means whereby I live."

Again, I believe that under any law which you can pass,
the Massachusetts Medical Society will have substantially
the controlling power in the board, unless you adopt the

doubtful expedient of providing that the members shall be limited to so many from each school, which I should question. I will not say it will be unconstitutional, but it would be open to very grave objections, and it is very doubtful whether you can prescribe limitations upon the appointing power of the executive, and say he shall appoint from one school and not from another. Why, look at the power of the Massachusetts Medical Society. The law of Massachusetts provides for medical examiners throughout the Commonwealth. We have got seventy-one in all, who were appointed by the Governor and Council. How many of them do you suppose belong to the Massachusetts Medical Society? Sixty-two, sixty-two! Now, I say that is a great tribute to the learning, to the intelligence and to the ability of the members of that society, and that learning and ability will give them the control of any board of examiners which may be appointed under any law, and they know it, and that is why they want the law. But that society was just as learned and just as able, and its members were just as honest and just as judicious when the people took away from it the power to regulate the practice of medicine in Massachusetts, as it is now, and the people do not want to put that power back into their hands, by direction or indirection. (Applause.)

Again, the bill purports to give the public competent and educated physicians, but it does not prescribe a course of examination which is of the slightest consequence with regard to the great branch of therapeutics. The Massachusetts Medical Society comes here and asks you to ordain that men may be licensed to practise medicine upon an examination in " anatomy, surgery, physiology, chemistry, pathology and obstetrics." Now, turn to the course which is required for admission into the Massachusetts Medical Society, " anatomy, pathological anatomy, physiology, general and medical chemistry, materia medica, therapeutics, midwifery, the theory and practise of medicine, clinical medicine, surgery, clinical surgery, hygiene and public hygiene." (By-laws of Massachusetts Medical Society.) Have these gentlemen ordained a course of examination for admission into their society which they regard as unnecessary to qualify a man to practise as a physician? By no means. They have adopted a full course, a wise course. And if we are to have any examinations at all, Mr. Chairman; if the people of Massachusetts are to have any legal band of medical men licensed to practise upon them, let them be licensed under an examination as full and thorough and complete as the Massachusetts Medical Society requires for admission into its own ranks.

Mr. Chairman, I believe that when doctors cease to make mistakes, when they cease to quarrel among themselves as they have before you, when they can control quackery within their own medical societies, and when they can keep members of their own societies from committing crimes for which they serve in the State prison and are hanged, it will be quite time for the medical gentlemen of the Commonwealth to ask that the issues of life and death in the practice of medicine and surgery shall be committed to the arbitrary decision of an irresponsible medical Star Chamber. (Applause.)

I have talked longer, sir, than I meant to talk. I have treated the subject in a very superficial and unsatisfactory manner to myself, but if I have opened any lines of thought which you, as wise and capable and judicious legislators, can pursue to a result which shall benefit, not the medical profession of Massachusetts, for they can take care of themselves, but the whole people of Massachusetts, I shall have answered the purpose for which I have spoken. I am much obliged to you for the courtesy with which you have listened to me. (Applause.)